# BLACK

# WOMEN

# WIN

**PUBLISHER**
**TA MEDIA**

www.PUBLISHYOURBOOKTODAY.INFO
WWW.PUBLISHWITHTIFFANY.COM

# Introduction

This anthology Black Women Win is not just another anthology. This anthology represents why black women are beautiful, strong, brilliant, and not to mention absolutely amazing.

The purpose of this book is to bring black women from all different walks and from all parts of the globe to write together and share their individual stories. These are stories of success, strength, trauma sharing these black women made it through. For years, there have been many black women who have lived through great sacrifices and celebrations that have been unseen, unheard, and swept under the rug for centuries. I say, we say "NO MORE HIDING".

In this masterpiece, we are proudly representing stories from black women across the globe. This is our time to collaborate and embrace greatness while we release our stories of success, business and increase to bless others. Black women have evolved and come a long way and it is time to celebrate us.

Each story is unique in its own way. Each story will capture your heart and pull you in to celebrate how we as black women are still winning after all we have survived.

We are thankful for each story, each testimony, and each moment of celebration. Black women have brought the essence of life back to the meaning of being brilliant and embracing a cultural evolution.

This first premiere volume of Black Women Win Anthology has set us on a path of greatness and gratitude. Read, enjoy and move forward.


Tiffany A Green-Hood

# Acknowledgments

As the visionary of Black Women Win Anthology, I would like to give honor and thanks to every co-author who has willingly shared their most precious stories with the world through this book. Without you, this publication would never be possible. I sincerely thank you, appreciate you and wish you all the very best in your businesses and your personal lives. May you live out every dream, aspiration, goal and gift with your name on it. The best is yet to come for you and all your dreams.

A huge thanks to Ebony Moody, Tonia "Ms. Tee" Taylor, Latoya Lyons, Kenya Bridges, Cheronda Hester, Ayana Bean, Alecia Tameko, Angela Eskridge, Monica Starks, Ramada Kaba, Keisha Allen, Lieasha Offord.

May your works produce unlimited wealth and greatness.

# Contents

# EBONY

# MOODY

# AMAZING GRACE
## EBONY MOODY

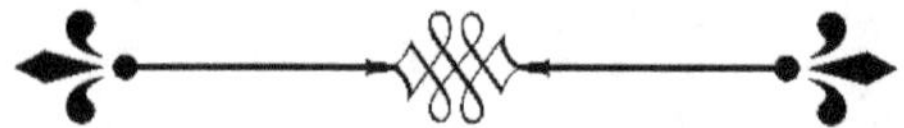

It was a crisp fall day in the Washington D.C. metropolitan area. As I turned on to I-395 headed to work, I retracted the top on my convertible and stepped on the gas. Even though the weather was a little cool, that didn't bother me at all. I loved the open road, hair blowing in the wind, speeding like I always did.

By most accounts I was winning in life. I had a great corporate career with amazing benefits, paid well and allowed me to travel frequently. I also had my own consulting business helping professionals transition their own careers. I purchased my dream car - a foreign convertible that could go from zero to 60 mph in 5.2 seconds. Everything seemed perfect. In reality, I was coming undone from the inside, out. I was a certified workaholic and a serial fixer; everybody's voice of reason, shoulder to cry on, prayer partner and loyal friend. Climbing the corporate ladder while trying to be everything to everyone, my health was spiraling down a dangerous path. I was 33 years old, so I thought I had time. I didn't notice the warning signs because I was laser focused on one thing- success.

It all started one year earlier.

"Miss Moody, your A1C is 8.5. I'm going to start you on 500mg of metformin first and see how that goes." My doctor announced vacillating between eye contact with me and typing notes. I looked down and saw the word 'diabetes' listed on my chart. My heart sank. For the first time in my life, I was disappointed in *me*. I remembered my grandmother religiously administering insulin with a needle twice a day, and her father before her doing the same. That's not how I envisioned my life or my future. But my eating habits were horrible. I ate out most days and when I did cook, I made red velvet pancakes, homemade yeast rolls, mac n' cheese... you know, the kind of food that is good for your soul, not your health.

I approached my diabetes like I approach most things - developed a strategy and took action. Medication was a prison sentence I would reject at all costs. I was determined to beat it. Over the next 90 days my eating habits changed drastically. I cut out all beverages besides water and black coffee. I ate vegetables and lean protein. I lost 30 lbs.

And then, life happened.

I got the call that my grandmother died on a Sunday afternoon in February. In that moment I felt like the four walls of my home had collapsed on top of me. My grandmother raised me as her own child. She was my biggest supporter, prayer partner and motivation. Everything took a back seat after her death. My health was no exception. The thought of living in a world without her felt dismal and scary. I'd had so many brushes with death that I was convinced my grandmother's favor with God and fervent prayers were the reason I was still alive. Without her spiritual covering I felt like I was living on borrowed time.

Keeping my head above the sea of grief was a silent struggle, the nagging fearing that I was next, not to mention managing the day-to-day personal and professional demands was exhausting, and I was losing. I kept a brave face for the world, but I was hurting emotionally and deep down I knew something was wrong physically, too. I was increasingly out of breath even when I was sitting still. Some nights I was so weak I would crawl to bed and other nights I didn't have the strength to do that. But I kept going, kept pushing myself until God literally sat me down one Sunday morning.

This particular Sunday started out no different from any other. I woke up, prayed, did my devotion and headed to church. Once I arrived in the church parking lot, I started feeling lightheaded and short of breath. Two women who were also heading to church noticed my carefully calculated steps across the parking lot and the disoriented look on my face. "Are you okay?" One of them asked. "I don't know…" I answered. The last thing I wanted was to be sprawled out in the middle of New York Avenue.

I made it inside the church, but each step felt like a sprint, and I was having a hard time breathing. Was I having a heart attack? I wasn't sure and even though I had felt this way before, this time felt different. Inside the sanctuary a friendly usher greeted me and pointed me in the direction of an available seat. By this time the entire sanctuary was swimming in my head. I couldn't take another step.

Then everything went black.

"Call an ambulance." I could hear someone say. An ambulance? Was this real? I had never been in an ambulance before. God knows how to get our attention and for me, passing out in the middle of Sunday morning service definitely did. I thank God for that wake-up call. After being released from the ER I made an appointment with my primary care physician, and this is what truly saved my life.

At my appointment, I recounted the episode to my doctor. She listened and used the stethoscope around her neck to listen to my heart and referred me to a cardiologist. The morning of my cardiology appointment I woke up lying on the floor in the foyer of my home. I couldn't remember if I'd laid there out of exhaustion or blacked out- again. By this time, I was declining. I could no longer walk up a flight of stairs, I couldn't stand for more than 10 or 15 minutes at a time, and everyday tasks like showering and getting dressed took me twice as long. I could no longer hide the fact that I wasn't well, the symptoms had become too frequent and too severe. I went to the bathroom and looked at myself in the mirror. My eyes were glossy and yellowish, one of them swollen from being pressed against the floor all night. This was a moment of reconciliation where how I felt inside matched how I looked on the outside; ill.

At the appointment a pleasant nurse guided me to the treadmill for a stress test. As soon as the treadmill inclined, sirens emitted from the computer connected to it. The nurse stopped the treadmill and reached for a phone bolted to the wall. The doctor came rushing in. A few minutes later he pulled a chair in front of me and sat down. "The monitoring device showed you had 26 cardiac episodes during the last week and the one you had today was very serious. You're going to need emergency heart surgery."

It's amazing how one word can change your whole outlook on life - surgery. Not just surgery, but heart surgery. I immediately began to pray. I also called my two prayer partners: my cousin Cheryl and my Ride-or-Die (ROD), Bishop Anita O'Brien. They both prayed and began to intercede on my behalf. God guided me to a Christian surgeon and less than a week later, I was headed to surgery. On the day of my procedure, I felt a great sense of peace. Somehow, I knew that God would see me through, and all would be well.

The procedure was scheduled for three hours which turned into four, which turned into six. Around that time the doctor came to speak to my family because the procedure wasn't going well. There was a significant amount of scarred tissue that led to complications. Ladies, this is why you need a prayer partner that can get a word through to heaven! I am blessed to have two and both were present during my surgery. When the doctor came out to deliver the news, they calmly told him to take a five-minute break then go back in and God would reveal the steps he needed to take.

The rest is history. When I came out of surgery, I couldn't move, I couldn't talk, I couldn't even open my eyes, but I could hear and knew I was alive. I was alive! To God be the glory! Over the next 30 days I made a full recovery. Health is truly wealth. God gave me a second chance to win; not accolades, degrees, prestige or even money. He gave me a second chance to live my best life and take charge of my

health, so I could win.

# TONIA "MS. TEE" TAYLOR

# GOD IS THE BEST PLANNER
## TONIA "MS. TEE" TAYLOR

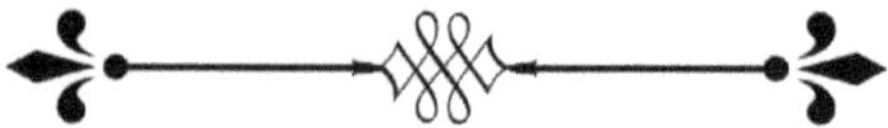

Growing up in Harlem exposed me to so many things. I came up in the 80's and 90's era and I must say I had a blast. I thought me and my family were middle class because we never went hungry, never wore secondhand clothes, and never wanted for anything. I realize we weren't middle class; my parents just made a way to make sure we didn't have to endure any of those things.

In my published memoir **_"HARLEM HEROINE"_** I wrote about my life growing up in Harlem and intentionally immersing myself into the street life of drug dealers and killers. I was a product of my environment and unfortunately these are the individuals I was attracted to. I decided to get into a life that I wasn't forced into. I sold drugs and had relationships with those that profited well from that life. I attracted those whose names were well known and respected in the street.

My upbringing was strict and full of love. My parents worked hard to provide for my sisters and me. My father was a strict Jamaican. My siblings and I grew up with good morals and ethics. I feared him yet I chose the street life whenever he traveled home to Jamaican, which he did often.

One thing I learned is that we as parents must instill good ethics and morals in our children. A little fear doesn't hurt either. Once that goodness is instilled, they will never forget those teachings. Although I indulged in that lifestyle, I never forgot those teachings from my parents.

We all have an idea of what we want our lives to be like. We have an idea of what the future may hold based off what we have planned out. Life doesn't always work that way because GOD has other plans; plans we may never understand unless we understand who GOD is.

My plan was to go to college for nursing and I did until I met my daughter's father who was really big in the streets. At 20 years old I thought I was rich, so school was no longer a priority. I was wrong. I dated him, got pregnant and before I knew it, he was going to jail for 23 years. I was left with 3 apartments, 2 cars, a van, and some money. I had all that, but what I lacked was the knowledge of what I could do with that money. I wish I knew about investing in Real Estate or stocks.

I always remember my father telling me how money was the root to all evil. In May of 1991 I found out how true that was. I was 3 months pregnant with a safe full of money when my brother-in-law stopped by to see me. Five minutes after he left, there was a knock on the door, and I opened it to find 3 masked individuals with guns. My fiancés brother set me up to be robbed. Although I had 3 guns to me head, I wasn't hurt thank GOD.

In 1994 I was shot by a crew that was down with one of my ex-boyfriend's crew. They came to my block to kill a friend I had grew up with. The beef had nothing to do with me. After yelling out one of the shooters names and then running off I was shot in my back, inches away from my spine. After seeing my friend fall in front of me, my life flashed in front of me. I could not leave my daughter here without any parents, so I got up and took myself to the hospital. The doctors said that had I laid there I would have smothered to death because I was bleeding internally. GOD wasn't ready for me yet.

I lost so many friends and loved ones to the street life and not once did it really hit me. I just chalked it up as a way of life that I was born into until the year 2000. That year I lost my brother Jermaine to the street life, and this is when I knew life had to be better than this. Selling drugs, witnessing murders, losing loved ones, and having meaningless relationships just for money and street status couldn't be what my life was supposed to be. I had never felt pain like that until my brother was taken. I had to ask GOD why all this pain and tragedy for one woman.

In 2005 I decided to put pen to paper to get this hurt and hate out of my heart. In 2008 I got on my knees and forgave the person who murdered my brother, which is something I had to do for me. It wasn't until 2015 that I published my writings of my life in Harlem and all the things that I had been through. I chronicled my life from 1985 to 2010. A documentary of my life was completed in 2019 that has now exceeded over 2.7 million views on YouTube. I never thought of becoming an author and a well-respected voice of the street. GOD changed the whole trajectory of my life. I didn't understand GOD's plan then, but now I do.

Now that I am the publisher of 5 books, I live my life encouraging my people to be better. I do that via my YouTube page, and I speak at lockdown facilities for the youth. This was GOD's plan for me. I understand the assignment. I am a God-fearing woman who strives to do his work. I am not perfect and never will be. Being perfect is not my goal. My goal is striving to always be better and helping others do the same.

My books and my documentary have encouraged more people than I could ever imagine. My supporters reach out to me from places that include New York, Scotland, Alabama London, West Africa and on. I am so thankful that I know what my purpose is. My life was saved to save others. My life story has gotten me on the Netflix documentary "CRACK" an exhilarating tale of how the government intentionally put drugs in low-income communities to destroy those less fortunate in the 1980's. I am also featured on BET's show "American Gangster-Trap Queens" season 3 episode 5. My story is a cautionary tale. I want to discourage my black women and men from an undesirable lifestyle that has been glorified and sensationalized.

I need my black men and women to know that no matter what you're going through, there is a reason for it. There's always a message in the mess. You must love yourself first. Have faith in GOD (if you believe) or that higher power. When you do, good things will begin to happen. We tend to want and expect validation from others when it's not needed. Your faith is enough. You are the one who will put in the work and the success will come. Building a relationship with oneself is one of the best relationships you'll ever have. No one matters, but you. This is the only way you will succeed in anything.

***Hebrews 11:1 Now, Faith is the substance of things hoped for, the evidence of things not seen.***

Manifest what you want, believe it and it will be. But remember GOD is the best planner. I allow the universe to do its thing. Sometimes we want instant gratification, and we want things now. As you have read earlier in this chapter, I started writing my book in 2005, but it wasn't published until ten years later in 2015. I was so glad that the universe had stalled my project because had my project been released any time before 2015, I'm not sure if all the great things that has happened would have.

No, I never finished Nursing school, but I did attain my bachelor's in business. I've been a licensed real estate agent for 17 years. I spent 8 years with an organization helping Veterans and those with mental illnesses obtain permanent housing. I was able to raise my daughter as a single parent. She was able to attain her 4-year degree. She is an IT specialist, owns her own home and makes six figures.

I live life with no regrets. Everything I went through was a lesson for me to learn from and to speak truth to others. If I had to go through all of that to save lives it was well worth it. It gives me great joy when parents reach out to me saying that they sit and watch my documentary with their children. It amazes me when black men tell me that when they think about going back to the streets, it's my story that humbles them.

I understand the assignment that was given to me. We all must use our life lessons to help others as well. Dig deep to figure out what your assignment is and do good works. It's up to us to help one another.

Don't worry. Stop fighting yourself. Have faith. Don't allow fear to stop you from succeeding.

The only way you will fail is by not trying. Just remember; For the battle is not yours, but GOD's. You can do it.  Ms. Tee

# RAMATA

# KABA

# DEFEATING MY GOLIATH
## RAMATA KABA

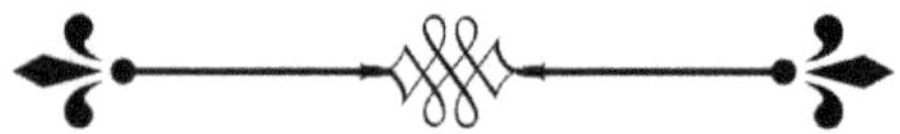

I believe we all have a goliath in our life that we must defeat in order for us to move on into our promise land. The promise land is a sweet land, here lies all your desires, wishes, aspirations, and happiness. We all have been assigned our very own personal goliath. When I use the word goliath, I'm referring to an obstacle/challenge/trauma/hurt that follows you around as you do this thing called life. Majority of us will encounter many goliaths along our way. I believe that we owe it to ourselves and the generations after us, to figure out what that specific goliath is in our life.

I've grown to know that the obstacle/challenge/trauma/hurt that is crippling you into thinking that you aren't good enough or you can't accomplish something is holding a lot of people back from showing up and operating as their very best self.

I came to learn about 1 of my goliaths about 3 years ago. I've encountered many obstacles and trauma in my day. Defeating this giant required me to have a lot of Faith, Strength, Discernment, and Isolation.

I want to take you back to about April 2020. I like to say I'm a Registered Nurse by trade Entrepreneur by heart. I've always enjoyed the thought of working for myself. I did what pretty much every millennial has been told to do. Go to school, get good grades, and get a good job. I followed and accomplished all of those "rules." For a short while I felt good, I graduated, and was working as a nurse in my dream hospital. That was my success and identity at the time. A few years later after this accomplishment, I suddenly started feeling very unfulfilled. I felt like there was more that I could be doing with my life and my abilities. I couldn't really explain it to people, and if I did, it seemed as though they didn't really understand what I was going through. This change of heart was something that only I could understand.

This was the start of my transition. Can I paint the picture for you?

Around this time, the whole world had just been introduced to an invisible virus that was killing many people. Everyone was frantic and in an uproar. No one knew what was happening. No one knew how severe this invisible virus was. Yet, something in me just woke up, and I knew that this was my bridge to freedom in some weird way. I decided to follow the pull. I took a leap of faith, packed up some of my belongings and ventured out to becoming a travel nurse. I figured that maybe this was my solution to my unhappiness and unfulfillment. Little did I know this leap of faith would turn into one of the best and most powerful decisions of my life.

After making this decision I entered a deep reflection period. As I was in my hotel room, that I was housed in, I would just cry, journal, and plead with God for answers.

I would ask questions like "What is my purpose in life?", "What am I supposed to be doing?" "Why am I here?"

Have you ever caught yourself pleading with God in such a way?

They say ask and you shall receive.

A few days later, before heading into work for my shift, the nurse manager called me on my phone and canceled my contract assignment earlier than expected. At first, I was taken aback, but I knew that hearing that news was nothing but the good Lord answering my plea.

I tried looking for other work immediately after the shock of being jobless had settled in. I kept hitting a brick wall it felt like, with no success. When you start feeling like things aren't moving fast enough, then it's time to be still, go within, and wait for direction.

I later packed up my things and headed back home. I had no clear blueprint or idea as to how I was going to make this happen, but I made an internal decision to not return to my then profession as a Registered Nurse. I made the decision to honor my heart, feelings, and to follow the pull. I made the decision to bet on myself. It all starts with deciding.

Many are called but few are chosen. I set out to walk this narrow path into entrepreneurship, not knowing how it would manifest for me. I planted my faith; at the time it was the size of a mustard seed because that was all I had to give God. I was really at one of the lowest times of my life mentally, spiritually, emotionally. I felt like I had been stripped away from my identity, the thing I used as a social badge of honor. Nursing is a prestigious profession. I decided to go against the status quo and follow my heart.

Once the initial shock wore away, after I made my decision. I was forced into a deep isolation period by God, whether I liked it or not. This was my wilderness season. During this season, I was re-learning myself, and God was purifying me and equipping me spiritually for my next level. Every new level comes with a new devil, and every new level requires a new you. Mentally.

I went on a 1-year sabbatical off the grid. I had access to very limited social media and limited outings; I was going through it. I was depressed and I felt like my identity was gone. I felt like I was being purged from all that I knew. I was re-learning myself, my desires. My faith was getting stronger by the day. I needed to go through this. I also was being purged from anything and anyone that was no longer meant for me.

This period of isolation for me was uncomfortable, it felt painful, and it was scary. I knew I was changing, I just had to be patient with God and the process. I had weeks where I didn't know where my next provision would come from, but on the outside looking in now, I realize that even if it was the 11th hour, at the very last minute, God always came through for me. I had no choice but to trust God. Again, on the outside looking in it was all by design. The only thing I needed to do was to trust the calling. God provided all the rest.

Yes, it was not always easy, and somedays you will not know how to move forward, but you must keep fighting and believing in your power within. If you keep at something persistently, it must work, it's inevitable.

During my wilderness season, I also set out to learn as much as I could on how to be a successful businesswoman. I became a sponge. I needed to be this teacher for myself because I didn't have an example of this person in my current physical environment. The term business, and all the jargon that comes along with business was all so foreign to me. I kept at it. I invested in courses, mentors, teachings, and really studied, as if I was study for a nursing exam. I had many trials and errors, invested a lot of time, money, and energy into learning about different industries so that I could be of service in a major way to these different companies.

Fast forward to about 3 years later present day 2022. I've went on to creating my own companies.

I am a black woman that is winning because I will never ever let my current circumstance define me. I am living proof that with faith even the size of a mustard seed, is all you need to join forces with God and start turning your dreams into a reality.

Being patient with your wilderness season is key. Don't rush the process. Every person that comes and goes is all a part of your story. Now, after seeing how resilient I am, I look forward to challenges, because I know with focus, and diligence nothing is truly impossible, and if I ever fail at a thing then I fail forward and continue to move forward.

Defeating this goliath in my life has been sweet. I am in my promise land. I feel powerful, and I look forward to inspiring more black women to move forward no matter what profession, or what you've been handed in life. Know that everyone has a story to tell. The best way that you can start approaching your goliath is by calling out the things in your life that you are unhappy with. Understand that it starts by identifying the issue. Once you identify the issue, make the decision to change, and once you make the decision to change, have faith the size of a mustard seed. Lastly get to work. Faith without works is dead!

# MONICA STARKS

# "FROM THE PROJECTS TO PROFESSOR
## MONICA STARKS

Onica's mouth always found herself in trouble during elementary school for talking too much. Her surname was Moore however, the second-grade teacher at the Catholic School nicknamed her Monica Mouth. I am she and she is I! Today I can laugh at that nickname because only God knew that I would be getting paid to talk as a public speaker and a college professor one day. What seemed like an impossibility to go from the projects to professor, is exactly what God blessed me to do. The path was not without twists and turns yet accomplished, nonetheless.

One and a half miles west of the Catholic School was the housing project that I lived in with my maternal grandmother. My parents separated, soon after, my mother was murdered, and my father thought it would be better for me to live with my maternal grandmother as he was raised by his grandparents. Existence at home sometimes felt like a war zone. There was a repertoire of behaviors one needed to develop to "take care of themselves" in the projects. (Anderson 1999) Similar behaviors were frowned upon at school. This was not just code switching this was behavior switching. There was a distinct difference between acceptable behavior at home and acceptable behavior at school.

Code switching has typically been known as switching between different languages or different ways of speaking. Many African Americans code switch when they are in professional settings amongst other racial groups however, it can be done amongst in-groups as well. Sociologists categorize groups where the members feel a sense of belonging, and loyalty as in-groups. I felt a sense of belonging to my friends in my neighborhood as well as my friends at school yet, when in each setting I often felt like an outsider or imposter. The children at the Catholic school were all African American but they were a different social class than my friends at home. They understood slang however, it was not used as much because we all were being taught to speak proper English, and most of them came from middle class families with two working parents.

Families paid full tuition to send their children to Catholic schools in the 1970's and 1980's which gave some people the assumption that those families "had money." The reality was that the families at the Catholic School simply had jobs which gave them a few extra dollars and they choose to spend it on their children's education, hoping to give them a better opportunity in the future. My family was no exception, we were not rich, my grandmother had a stable job for the first time in her adult life that she earned a salary and not hourly wages as she did while raising her children. There was no real goal for me just that we were members of the church and there was extra money in the household so why not send me to the school and give me a good education. I was expected to do well and pass every grade level. My grandmother warned me not to waste her money. There was no real expectation of maintaining a good grade point average just that I could not fail. My expectations came from the assumption I had of what my neighborhood peers thought of me. After school everyone in the neighborhood hung out and were not in study groups or extracurricular activities so to fit in, I thought I needed to be available to hang out, so I drifted away from the girl scouts and basketball team I was involved with at school.

High school was my first introduction to school with Caucasian students. The only interaction I ever had on a personal level with Caucasian people was with my stepmother, whom by this time I had not seen for about five years. The last thing I wanted to do was go to another Catholic school for high school and I really did not want to go to an all-girl school, but my grandmother would not bend and allow me to go to the co-ed public high school in walking distance from our apartment. The Catholic school was two city busses and a rapid transit ride away from my home. I had assimilated to fit in with the neighborhood friends, assimilated to fit in with the middle-class peers in elementary school and now I will have to assimilate to fit in with the Caucasian students at my new high school. My identity was distorted because I was just trying to fit in everywhere and never determined who or what I really wanted to be. No mother, no father, no siblings, attempting to be hood enough to protect myself and fit in at home, attempting to be cultured enough to fit in with the middle-class families in elementary school and learning to socialize with different races in high school. There was so much work involved in all those things that I could not spend any time finding myself or dealing with the trauma that was accumulating inside of me.

Teenagers that have little to no adult restrictions make their own decisions and, in most cases, they are not the best decisions. I made decisions at this point that fit the narrative of the facade I had begun to live. Home life was winning over school life. I enjoyed school because it was a break from the monotony and the relationships, I was developing were different. They were easy, but at home I was able to live like an adult and at school

I was treated like a child (because I was a child.) I did not like that. My friends and I enjoyed partying which included underage drinking and smoking pot. Once you begin this regimen it is difficult to stop. I believed it was fun. I thought I was carefree and most of all I was not a bump on a log, I easily fit in with my peer group. My lifestyle was masking the trauma and pain boiling inside of me.

"We wear the mask that grins and lies,

It hides our cheeks and shades our eyes, —

This debt we pay to human guile.

With torn and bleeding hearts we smile,"

-Paul Laurence Dunbar,

Graduation was an expected completion of the goal and in my family it was enough. Most of my friends at school were headed to college and I was interested in college when I was around them and I even applied to a few colleges and was accepted into them all. There are some downfalls to being middle class when it comes to financial aid, your family is expected to pay some of the tuition at most colleges.

My family was not prepared to do this so I had to tell myself I would wait to go to college, but I would go so that I could one day get out of the projects that we still lived in. Somewhere deep inside of me I believed that. I enjoyed the times that I was able to go visit with my friends from school in the suburbs, I coveted their lives, and would tell myself that one day I would live in a house with carpet and two levels.

As happy as I was partying at home with my friends I dreamed of those small things and envisioned myself living differently. I was so lost in my home lifestyle that I was not making any strides towards upward mobility; I was stuck. I got pregnant by a young man from the neighborhood that landed himself in jail and left me alone to raise our son. He convinced me to marry him because of our son and I did not realize at the time that I was slowly moving further away from the life of my dreams, I was losing. So much for the better life I was supposed to have because of the twelve years of Catholic School education.

A Metamorphosis needed to take place and one day I woke up, frustrated and filling worthless so I registered for classes at the Community College which was 0.7 miles from my apartment. That was the beginning of the rest of my life! School had a different meaning to me this time around. I was on a mission toward upward mobility and not simply going to school because I had to by law or because my friends were going. Change is a process, and I did not walk through the doors of the college and become a new person however, my mindset was transforming. As I met likeminded people and built relationships with faculty and staff members at the college, I had less desire to hang out partying and more desire to connect with people that were living the type of life I longed for. First thing I had to do was commit myself to God and develop a church life that kept me grounded with the faith I was taught as young girl. The second thing was I had to divorce the low life husband. The third was I had to be a sponge and soak up all that I was learning outside of the classroom. Fourth, I had to move out of the projects and fifth, continue my post-secondary education.

Check, check, check, check and check. Some of the things on this makeshift check list were easier than others, some took years, but I accomplished them all. Over the years my mindset and outlook changed. I wanted a middle-class life for myself and my son, I did not want him to ever have to live like I did and never suffer the way that I did financially in his adult life. I wanted him to feel like the girls I went to high school with, safe and content. I did not want him to think that smoking pot and drinking was cool or something he needed to do to mask the trauma and pain he was living like I did. One monkey wrench was thrown at me as I was on my upward climb and that was a diagnosis of End Stage Renal Failure at twenty-seven years old.

I started winning. I completed my education at the Community College with an Associates of Arts degree and transferred to Tiffin University and earned a bachelor's degree of Business in Organization Management and finished up at

Cleveland State University and earned a master's degree in Sociology. The Master's Degree afforded me the opportunity to become a Sociology professor at the same Community College I attended and earned my Associates Degree one semester after graduation. I teach many students that are in similar situations as I was in when I registered for college. I am relatable because I share with my students that I am an alumni that lived 0.7 miles East of the campus in the projects and I wanted change, I earned it, and they can too. I made the Dean's list as a student at the community college and in graduate school I was inducted into the international honor society for Sociology as a lifelong member. I fulfilled a long-term dream of writing my story of being diagnosed with End Stage Renal Failure which is a form of chronic kidney disease and became a published author! When I type my name in on Amazon.com I see my book, how awesome? I would have never imagined that I would accomplish any of these things when I was eighteen years old.

I am winning today because I wanted to win! I eliminated what I knew was holding me back, I changed my mindset and outlook on life, I married someone new, I had two daughters with him, I am a college professor, an author, a motivational speaker, a grandmother, an advocate for chronic kidney disease and a happy well rounded human being! Yes, I am winning. Black women do win, it may sometimes be difficult for us initially, but we do win.

"I don't think of myself as a poor deprived ghetto girl who made good. I think of myself as somebody who, from an early age, knew I was responsible for myself, and I had to make good." Oprah Winfrey

Works Cited

Anderson, E. (1999). *Code of the Street: Decency, Violence and the Moral life of the Inner City* (1st ed.). W.W. Norton and Company.

Paul Laurence. Dunbar, ""We Wear the Mask."" from The Complete Poems of Paul Laurence Dunbar. (New York: Dodd, Mead and Company,)

# KENYA
# BRIDGES

# "MY SUCCESS STORY"
## KENYA BRIDGES

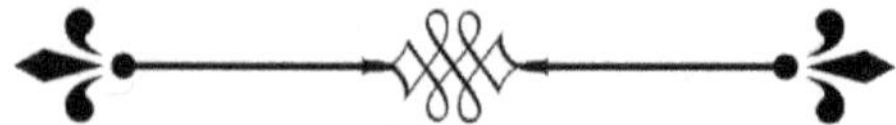

2014! That was the starting point of discovering my emotional needs, fears, and self-judgments. Through that, it allowed me to access pieces of myself that seemed inaccessible. I started having strong desires to be in tune with finding a serious spiritual grounding defining what love was for me. Certain things during a span of eight months could have destroyed me. When going through the process of unveiling and mending and stripping away old behaviors and beliefs, I've learned that there is power, and rewards discovered. So have a seat and let me tell you what occurred.

Spring 2014, I was in my fifth semester of college. I found myself wanting something meaningful to manifest into my life. So, I tested my spirit by becoming celibate. I made an agreement with myself to do three-month increments. In this agreement, I was to add three months if I didn't meet someone worthy to ending agreement, I was to add three more months. Well, I met someone.

What was special about my choosing him to end my first three months of abstinence was the lack of pressure when I told him. He wanted to end all communication, but I was the one that applied pressure to his reluctance. However, our encounter didn't happen until those three months were over. Spirit must've known that my abstinence was a serious commitment. My cycle had made her grand appearance and delayed all plans until further notice. Even though it was a brief sexual encounter, it was a starting point of my quest.

Before the end of the semester, I made the decision to take up some classes during the summer. Those were some I'd dropped some semesters prior and a few in my major. I ended up reconnecting with a guy I've known for some time. Something was different about and it was the information and him exposing himself to some truths about our world and religion. To be brief, I was very intrigued by the knowledge. Finally, conversations that weren't surface level. This stirred up misconstrue feelings for him. Our moment was short lived, but I discovered something about myself. I had a love language of sharing knowledge.

One night in my dorm room I laid crying. Crying for I don't know how long but I know it was a prayer for love. A love to have someone I can share what I know without feeling weird and judged. A love that goes beyond the surface. I was so tired of attracting certain dynamic relationships I'd allowed into my life. Those flooding emotions came over me quick but unbeknownst to me, that love had been growing for four months. I assumed I was bloated due to how much I was eating and all of the gas I had.

I refused to accept the idea of pregnancy. I wasn't on birth control for years and I hoped someone would say if the condom broke. My roommate suggested for weeks to just go ahead and purchase a test. Finally, I submitted; standing in that bathroom with a pregnancy test at 21 years old was the last thing I imagined I would be doing at that time.

Seeing those two blue lines on four tests felt like a dream or a movie. I was an art major, so there were moments when I had to lift heavy objects. The overwhelming thoughts of have a miscarriage not knowing I was pregnant made me so sad. My only concerns were finding out the health of my baby. After those thoughts subsided, I hurried to tell the young man my spirit led me to reveal we were about to have a child.

After that conversation, so much had gone through my head in a matter of minutes. How was I going to tell my family, where was I going to live, work, what was I going to do about school. It was just so much I had to figure out before the Fall semester started. Even though my mind was on 10, I knew I had to find a doctor and insurance immediately for myself and my child. On one hand I was excited to share my love with this child, and on other hand I was feeling isolated. There I was pregnant, not knowing who the dad was, in school, living in a dorm and working two jobs. It was so hard. The only thing that kept me going was the movement of my unborn.

I had to embrace these new challenges head on but still uncertain. Working two jobs sometimes in one day was unbelievable. I worked on campus which I was fortunate to be able to have that convenience. This allowed me to be able to work in-between classes. I did my work study in the library and Subway was right up the street. Imagine me big, pregnant feet and rushing to class or work! My worst day honestly was getting off late and having to walk back to the dorm. That was up the street as well but at night the emotions drowned me. I was 21 years old, pregnant, living in a dorm and having to walk back and forth to work. However, me and my unborn child along with my shameful tears were worth it.

The support of my coworkers at Subway uplifted me. Especially James. James's heart was so genuine and beautiful. We were always able to have good conversation and laugh. My other coworker, with her Jamaican accent and realness was pure. I am glad I let them in because I needed nearby support. One of the unknown fathers at the time wouldn't even acknowledge me. The end of the semester was a long way, but I had to arrange ending the semester early. Professors were willing to let me complete my art projects and any papers before the Thanksgiving break. Another professor let me turn in a nine-page paper in for the spring semester. That assignment was my biggest relief because even though I would deliver my baby in December she would still be small enough that I can still focus my paper and studying.

That entire year was a sudden change for me mentally, emotionally and deeply in spirit. Having to learn to balance working two jobs, school, planning to move back to New Orleans and my own thoughts of living in a dorm while pregnant had to be done regardless of how much shame I placed on myself. My spirituality was strong because through all of it, I'm surprised that I didn't give up. My schedule was crazy. I would be back home from work at midnight and wake up at 7AM for work the next day. The embarrassment I felt having to eat in the cafeteria was dreadful. I would cry and rub my baby thinking I'm grateful she chose me.

Looking back, I used to cry about that entire situation but now I'm glad that I went through it. I eventually returned back to school although I didn't finish. I told a coworker I didn't know who my daughter's dad was. She looked at me with tears because she went through it to and was so shameful, she continued to carry it. She looked me in my eyes and told me she was glad I was so open to share that with her. Living through my ups and downs reminds me that I can do anything no matter the hardships may come to me. I can face them without shame and embarrassment.

# AYANA

# BEAN

# "A YEAR AND A DAY"
## AYANA BEAN

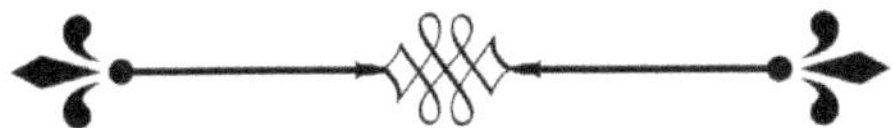

**P**overty, single motherhood, and homelessness are some of the social factors that lead to the rising number of women in prison. Women in prison have experienced victimization, unstable family life, and substance abuse, which has led to poor decision-making. Patience, faith, and wisdom from the lessons learned, can lead to a brighter tomorrow. I am Ayana Bean, and I am telling my story of going from the darkness of prison to the shining light of a businesswoman.

Although there were ignored traumas in my life at an early age, there was still a burning desire in me to excel to the moon. Oftentimes the feelings of sadness and depression would prevent me from moving forward but I knew there would be more for me in life if I just get to the bottom of it. Remove the heavy weight from my mind, clear it out. When I started thinking like that a wave of fear took over me. I was afraid to face the truth of my traumas and the aftermath of the destruction they had caused in my life but in order to move forward, you must go back and face the facts. Where do I begin?

**LOSS**

I was the ultimate Daddy's girl. Why was that? Just me, Mom & Dad for 5 years until my baby sister Shani came. Oh, how I loved my dad. He was the best thing in the world. Was he really? To me, yes. Was he what a man should show his daughter how she should be loved by a man? There is a yes and no to that question. I felt loved by my parents. I saw them love each other. I saw my mom work hard, go to school and be a wife that made a home with her husband and children. My Dad worked too. We had family fun, went to the movies, out shopping and enjoying our little family time. This was love and in fact all the love I wanted to exist. Confusion and pain hit me when I saw my dad and another woman looking like he loved her like I saw him love mom. This wasn't right. Mom was only at work so how could he love someone that fast. Why was he so mad at me when I told mom? He blamed me and spanked me before mom arrived home from work. They called each other bad names that I was never supposed to repeat. He took his hands and used them as weapons on my mom in front of my little eyes. That wasn't the love we shared. After that day Dad was gone from us and I always thought he was gone to the woman I saw him love while mom was at work. I was pain feeling the loss of my dad and acted out for many years and although as I got older and was able to see him again. I never recovered from the loss of my dad.

## SECRETS

Playing house was a favorite of mine to do with my favorite cousin. We would always be sisters and I would be the big sister because I was older than her by 2 weeks. I was also way smaller than her. In fact, I was so tiny my Grandaddy named me Lil Bit. All my family called me that. One day our favorite game of playing house added a new person and he changed our lives forever. He said that we could playhouse with him, and he would be the dad and that sounded great to me because I sure missed my dad, and every house should have a dad. Now we need to find a mom because we are sisters, and we need a mom and a dad we thought. He said, "you be the mom, and you be the daughter." I was confused why was she able to be the mom and I had to be the daughter? She was the youngest, not me and I don't want her telling me what to do. Was this jealousy? I felt less than her. I always felt like a big girl before that day. I was the oldest sister, niece, cousin, granddaughter, and daughter. I'm supposed to be the mom. Mom is the boss. My cousin was so happy to finally be the big girl and be able to tell me what to do. Then playing house began. He made us lay down next to each other and unzip our pajamas. Then he began to touch us where nobody was supposed to touch. I squeezed my eyes close until playing house was done. Playhouse Dad said "you can never tell anybody about this, or you will be in trouble. When something hurts inside, smile brighter it makes the pain go away. This is how I learned to smile through secret pains.

## POWER

Discovering myself hasn't been a smooth ride. Challenges have not stopped coming my way and my response to challenges have not always worked out in my favor. I became a teenage mother, battled domestic violence from a drug addicted partner, served jail time in both the state and federal prison systems for financial fraud. In fact, my federal prison sentence is where I began to face the fears and pains of my past traumas. I was embarrassed and ashamed of being a convicted felon. Released from federal prison in 2014 I started working at an all-women's gym and figured I'll just work my way up and hide forever. I received a call from BET Network to feature my story about the financial crimes I committed. Hiding was my plan but not God's plan for me. God didn't want me to hide behind shame and embarrassment. He has groomed me all along and prepared me to stand tall and be an example for those who wanted to hide and give up just like me. Just when I thought he was through with me is when I saw how he was just getting started with me. Today I'm featured on BET American Gangster Trap Queens and using the platform to encourage other women who hide behind their shame, guilt, and embarrassment. I wrote a book about my life and all the pains in it. I became a best-selling author. I gained strength. I made an agreement with myself that I wouldn't be afraid of being the smartest person in the room, no need to fit in, no seat at the table needed as I carry my own table and chairs. Fearless Bean is what my name should be changed to. I made the decision that nothing would determine who this young black woman would be but me.

My journey has been a great learning experience for me. I didn't believe I was strong, but I was able to make it through abuse, shame, insecurity, and prison.

I started with ordinary dreams. I learned to braid hair in the 7th grade and had dreams of being a hairstylist. In high school, I started learning business finance and accounting, and I loved that too, so I figured I would own a business someday. However, I moved too quickly.

I craved independence, which brought on significant responsibility. When that got tough, I made poor decisions that were criminal. After making it through prison, I no longer think the same, want the same, or believe the same. I matured and was able to heal my internal wounds.

When I went through childhood dysfunction, abuse, and imprisonment, I felt like I wouldn't make it, but because I focused on myself, my faith, and my freedom, I believe I am successful today.

I was able to turn my past problems into positive actions. I decided to make a start by putting skin in the game. I started reaching out to city counselors and other organizations to see where there was a need. Lastly, I started my nonprofit organization, A YEAR AND A DAY FOUNDATION, a transitioning program for felons re-entering society. As a Philanthropist, I am now able to give back and make a positive difference.

I hope my story will help other women and men. I pray that my story will be used as a cautionary tale that can encourage others to have patience with themselves and always to know that the best thing to do is the right thing.

# CHERONDA L. HESTER

# LOOK UP, YOU WIN
## CHERONDA L. HESTER

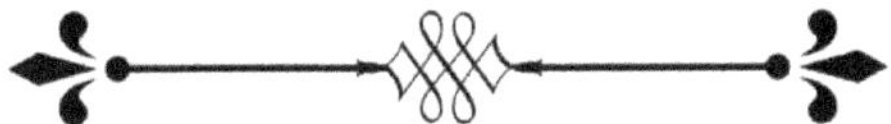

While growing up in Gary, Indiana, which is about 30 minutes from the windy city known as Chicago, I could not help being surrounded by sports fanatics. The love felt for the Chicago Bulls, Bears, White Sox and Cubs was undeniable. Whether you sat in the stands to see the Cubs play at Wrigley Field, listened to the game broadcasted over the radio or watched them on your television during the 7th inning you heard the song, "Take Me Out to The Ballgame". The last line in the song always gathered fan enthusiasm – "For it's one, two, three strikes, you're out, At the old ball game".

In baseball, depending on the number of strikes a team receives helps determine which team is statistically likely to win or lose the game. And in life, most people associate the phrase "three strikes" to mean they are out…out of opportunities, options and optimism.

Unfortunately, we live in a world where people are always reminding you about what you have done wrong or have not done. Then they try to predict what will happen to you in the future based on their terms, tendencies, and traditions.

Statistics or "stats" is defined as the theory, methods and practice of forming judgments about the limitations of a population. The reliability of statistical relationships is typically based on random sampling. Random sampling? Nothing about me or you is random. In fact, I know that I am fearfully and wonderfully made in the apple of God's eye. I had to learn and understand that no matter what I had done, not done, or thought about doing, God's plan cancelled out, disrupted, and disputed any statistics society tried to use to label and limit me. Should you consider society statistics when it comes to your life?

If I had considered the statistic of being a black girl born and raised in Gary, Indiana, a city primarily known for three things - Michael Jackson and the Jackson Five, United States Steel Mill, and earning the notorious title of becoming the murder capital of the United States, I would have become an entertainer, a thirty-year mill worker, or possibly been a victim of violence. I would not have allowed myself to truly experience the gift of God's plan designed for my life.

I was born in a two-parent home where my parents were married and very well off. Society would say I had it all. Two loving and hardworking parents, lovely home, living in a great neighborhood, loving family and plenty of friends. For some, many would say my upbringing was the ideal situation. Well, as time passed, my great two-parent home turned into a one-parent home. Like most children, the trauma caused by separation did something to me. Traumatized, I started looking for love in all the wrong places. During that time, I found myself settling without even noticing it in different situations. Because I was afraid of feeling the pain I felt when my parents separated, I started to compromise who I was to avoid experiencing the same pain. I did not realize I was just adding another layer of negative emotions one on top of the other.

To society, this was strike one!

Growing up my mom did everything she could to make sure we did not become a statistic. I remember her being what I thought was overprotective, but now I am extremely grateful for it. I went from always having a babysitter to not being able to spend the night at my friends' house. Then not being able to go everywhere with everybody at any given time, no matter what was going on. Missing church was not an option. On the Sundays my mom had to work, she would send me to church with my grandmother. I still remember the Sunday I gave my life to the Lord and being baptized. Giving my life to Christ, I thought everything would become better. I thought to myself, dad is about to come home, and mom is about to be happy again. Sadly, that was not the case. Dad was still out of the house and mom was still working to make ends meet but, I still had hope. Unlike most homes where parents have separated, thankfully my dad was still present. He made sure that while he dealt with his own life, he did not become a stranger to mine.

Before I knew it, I was getting ready to enter high school. Honestly, I had hoped life would look differently. I thought the days of waking up early during the school week to sit at my aunt's home until the school opened, while my mom went to work, were behind me. Once I turned sixteen, I planned to drive and drop my brother and sister off at their school before I headed to mine. I also thought I would no longer have to walk home from basketball games. I had convinced myself that things were going to be great.

I loved to watch the movie Grease seeing them have dances, basketball games and fun. So, when I entered high school, I expected a Grease experience, but it was more like scenes from the Lean on Me movie. We had fights multiple times a day. Garbage cans werc set on fire. Classmates were here one day and gone the next. In high school, I never expected my number one concern to be safety. I remember walking home from a basketball game and in the school parking lot I was pushed to the ground by my cousin to shield me from a shootout. My reality did not mirror my desires, and something had to change. In my mom's bedroom at fourteen years old, I gave my life to Christ all over again. I remember reminding God of His word...His promises, and I realized I had not been the best. I did not allow my shortcomings to keep me from asking God for forgiveness and starting over. I knew as a new believer I had just as much right to His word as an old believer.

Still young and full of hope, I believed things were about to look up. In my junior year, my rock passed away. My grandfather was the rock that helped hold my mom and dad up. Where my dad fell short, my grandfather was always there to pick up the slack. It was a very challenging experience but, I made it through.

Entering my senior year of high school, I found out the one thing that was consistent was changing... and I was devastated. I learned that we had to move out of our family home. Although my mom worked multiple jobs, it was still not enough to keep us in our home. We had to move from a 2,464 square foot home, where we had two kitchens, multiple bathrooms, and we each had our own bedroom, to an 846 square foot home. There we had one kitchen, one bathroom and my siblings and I shared a bedroom. Not to mention we did not have any friends in this neighborhood. As always, my mom did her best to make sure we did not become a statistic. Regardless of where we lived, she would always make the house a home. She gave us instructions and shared her wisdom about keeping ourselves for marriage, respecting our temples and honoring ourselves. Along with keeping us surrounded by great people. But as you know regardless of how great our parents and families are, we still must choose to listen to the direction and wisdom given. How many of you know I did not always listen to those great directions? Due to my lack of following instructions, I found myself nineteen, unmarried, pregnant, and about to drop out of college.

Strike two!

Now, I am about to become a mom. I really had to take a moment and think about life and not just my own. So, like most, I thought about everything my mom and dad tried to teach me. Along with the promises of God I got to the point I desired to live a Christ like life. At the age of nineteen, I began that Christ focused journey. I am sure many of you know that through this transition, I lost friends and even some family stopped coming around. They would call me Jesus jr. or would say she thinks she is better than us. But I did not allow that to stop me from desiring better or from following Christ. I continued to do what I knew was right. As you know I did not always get it right and I still do not now. I did learn that I will never be perfect, but I do serve a perfect God!

Fast-forward a few years later, I found a job, got married, was pregnant again, and went back to school. I thought life was great! I was determined to live out the prophetic words that had been spoken over me. I had just given birth to baby number three, then it felt like my life was hit by a ton of bricks. My marriage began to take a turn for the worst. Have you ever been told something great, believed it, and then suddenly your life reflects the opposite of what you were told?

Strike three… divorce!

Society and statistics have a way of making you feel horrible. Thinking the worst in every situation, automatically causes stress and frustration. Wondering will anything ever go right...what others would think or say? Finally, getting past my emotions and the opinions of others, I came to the realization with who and what mattered most - God, my children and me. It was time for me to try and look up and see that my latter would be greater than my before. Have you ever felt so low you could not see your way up?

**Black Woman**, I want to remind you to **LOOK UP, YOU WIN!** No matter how hard it may seem, better is coming! Today I am a woman who is a believer, wife to an amazing man, mom to seven wonderful children, daughter, sister, aunt, author, CEO, nurse, hairstylist, certified life coach, senior leader in ministry, and a serial entrepreneur, I am proof that your past does not dictate your future. Be encouraged, and know regardless of statics, opinions of others, or even your past mistakes, you still win. Society tells us three strikes and you are out, but as you can see society does not determine your end. You do! Black Women, remember your choices determine your current destination. Society is not the author of your life, God is. He is the author and the finisher, and according to His word, you win! So do not worry about what the other authors/publishers are saying your book has been written.

So, if you still have not figured it out, you win! You won before you got started. It is about you going through your process. No battle is too hard. God has never lost a battle, nor has he wasted one and he is not about to start now!! Be grateful for where you are today and know that God is not through with you yet!

# LATOYA LYONS

# "DON'T BELIEVE EVERTHYING YOU THINK"

## LATOYA LYONS

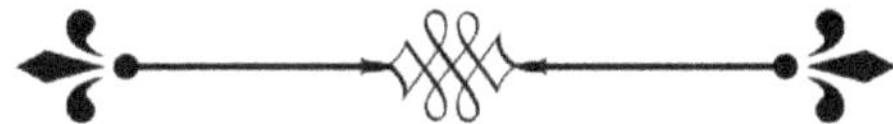

It is so easy for us to discredit ourselves, to believe the negative over the positive. There are fears that live within us that are not true, but we have begun to believe that they are true. Why is it so hard to believe that we are great? Our past should not determine this.

Dear me, I love you never forget that. You are beautiful and deserving of all the love in the world. Do not expect others to give what they do not know how to give and do not be disappointed when you do not get what you expect. Do not put your expectations on others because they will let you down every time. Did that statement resonate with you? Did you feel it because when I wrote it, it was random but at the same time I felt I needed to say it to myself. I needed to hear those words. I believe we don't love ourselves enough. So many times, we love others more than we love ourselves, yet we don't want to disappoint others. We love our family, we love our spouses, we love our children, we love our friends, we even love our jobs. Most times they disappoint us or let us down in some way. Growing up as a child I learned to put my trust in other people but as an adult I quickly learned that you cannot trust everyone. I want to share two experiences in my life that allowed me to own who I am. It is important to understand that everything you go through is empowering in some way and there is always a lesson to learn.

**For Better or for worse.** What does that statement really mean? Maybe after you hear my story you will understand it a little better. Hi, my name is Latoya Clark Lyons and before I was tested by God, I never knew the true meaning of the vow "for better or worse". Let me take you back to my childhood to give you a glimpse of my mind set now. I grew up with my mom and dad for most of my life and their closeness showed me the kind of marriage I wanted. We all know we want to get married when we are young but not just get married but to start a family and build a foundation with a man who I loved and would love me back. Boy, I had no idea that did I not know what love was. You think especially when your young that love is just feelings and as long as you have those feelings, your world will be ok.  I am here to tell you; love don't pay no bills. When God decided to test me, I had been married 5 years and believe me it was not easy to get to that point.

I remember the first time I met my husband. We both worked together and my first opinion of him was what a geek. I had no idea how charming he would be. We dated in 97, it was fun, and we had so much in common. We liked music, video games, sex, and talking. Joseph, I can say is my best friend even till this day. We dated for a year and then I was pregnant with Lil Joe. My first thought was to get married because I was always taught not to be just another girl with a baby daddy. I was another girl with a baby daddy because he had no intention of getting married or even settling down with me. He knew he would take care of his child but not be married to me or anyone else for that matter. It wasn't until 2002 that we finally tied the knot, but a lot happened in between. I can remember after I had my baby and telling his daddy we can't live together anymore. He wanted to do what he wanted to and that was hard and took too much strength out of me. I realized that regardless of what anyone says, having a baby with a man creates a bond that is unbreakable. You will always have a connection to them for the rest of your life.

We got back together in 2001 and talked about marriage but there was always a money issue. I decided since everything was going to be about money to just go to the courthouse and get married. On 9/20/02 at 2:30 pm we said I do. I remember it was one of the happiest days of my life. We spent the weekend together at a hotel in the city for our honeymoon. We all know about the better but what happens when the worse creeps in.

Fast forward April 2007, I found out my husband cheated on me. I felt like all was lost and I was also 5 months pregnant with our third child. I did not know who I was without him. All I had been for the time were together was a wife and a mother. I lost Latoya at this point I did not even know how to find her. I was totally lost. I felt like God didn't love me and I wanted to die. It was hard going through this, but I can remember God holding me and showing me, everything would be okay. I knew it would not happen overnight, but I knew one day. It was hard trusting that God would see me through, or that I would even survive. It wasn't just me I had to think about. I had two kids and one on the way. One thing my counselor would always say to me was that you don't go through things for yourself you go through for other people so that they have someone to relate to and can draw strength from your experience. I think the best statement she ever made was "the tunnel maybe dark but there is light at the end, but you have to keep moving in order to get to the light". It does not have to be big steps it can be baby steps and they do not have to be many they can be a few. Just keep moving or inching toward the light. So, that is what I did every day I got up. I had to be strong for my two sons and provide a life from them. I never wanted them to see me weak, so I would never cry in front of them. I did cry every night, but a voice would always say after that "Okay you got that out now what?", What are you going to do now? I think my wake-up call for this situation was when I almost lost my daughter. I was losing weight instead of gaining because I was not eating. After that happened, I set goals. I vowed to get my Certified Professional Coder certification and publish a book.

Always remember, work will not love you back and you can be replaced. One thing I have personally learned over the years is that a job does not care about your well-being. At least not the jobs I have worked. There are jobs that will give you PTO but do not expect you to really use it. I do not believe in asking for time off but rather informing the job that I will be taking time off. There have been so many times that I have been miserable on a job. I would wake up and dread going or get there and count the seconds until it was time to get off. Work is hard to do when you're not happy where you are.

Understand this statement, the job you have is not the only job you are qualified to get. Just like you got this one, you can get another one. Sometimes we are under the impression that we are lucky to have a job and the reality is that they are lucky to have you. You bring something to the table that no one else can bring. Remember, out of all the people they interviewed they called you back and offered you the job. I have come across so many people who have said I cannot afford to lose this job, or I might get fired. Both statements are true but, just because they are true does not mean you have to be stuck where you are in a job that is going nowhere or where you are miserable. You might lose this job or get fired but the qualifications that allowed you to get this job will allow you to get another one. You must trust and believe that the skills and knowledge you have can get you any job that you want and if you don't have the skill, you can learn it. Never put limits on yourself or allow others to put limits on you. The point is your current job is lucky to have you and if you feel they do not appreciate you find another job that does. Let me tell you my story. Please I repeat, please do not follow my example I have never been at a job longer than 3 years unless it was a contract where I controlled my time. Controlling my time is essential to me because it allows me to travel and accomplish other things in a day and not necessarily be confided to a set time such as a 9-5 but still get the job done if that makes sense. I have personally gotten bored easily in a job because I was not being challenged. If I feel I'm not growing in a position, or I am not allowed to grow than it's time to go. Let me share a time in my life when I literally begged God to let me get fired. The year was 2012 and I had just completed my bachelor's degree in Healthcare Administration. I wanted to utilize my skills in a different way and do something I had never done before. I accepted a job as an auditor at a third-party administrator. It was new fun and exciting. I'm sure we have all had a job like this that challenges us in the beginning. Part of my job was writing others up for errors that have made to ensure that these same errors were not made going forward. With this new position, came issues. Those issues were nothing I could not handle. I mean I looked at it like a bunch of gossiping girls upset because they had to be told they did something wrong. The issue that I had with this job was that you could never take time off. Prior to this job I worked part-time as an instructor and medical biller for my own company, so it was an adjustment. The environment became tense, and the turnover rate was high. Fast forward 1 year and 3 months to the day, I was fired or how they like to say laid off. I worked all day because most jobs allow you to work the whole day before letting you go.

At the end of the day my supervisor came to my desk and said we needed to go to human resources. As we rode the elevator there was an awkward silence no words were spoken. We got to the human resource office and the representative seemed tense as well. She began to speak and said because you were absent for being sick, we are going to have to let you go. I thanked her this was a blessing in disguise. I decided to reach out to doctor's offices to get new clients under my business. This experience showed me that I did not want to work a 9-5 and with a little effort I can build my own business. The client I obtained after losing this job helped me to learn the different talents that I possessed.

Always remember God has the final say in all things. Own who you are never attach yourself to a person, place, company, or organization, but instead attach yourself to a mission, a calling, or a purpose. If you do this, it allows you to keep your power & peace. I cannot agree with this more.

Black Women, I pray that my story has inspired someone that they too can make it through any obstacle that tries to deter you from reaching your goals and living the life you know is promised to you. Each person's journey is unique and different, much like the stories in this book. As this resonates, know what's best for you and what's not for you, then go and be gr eat.

# ANGELA ESKRIDGE

# SELF-WORTH
## ANGELA ESKRIDGE

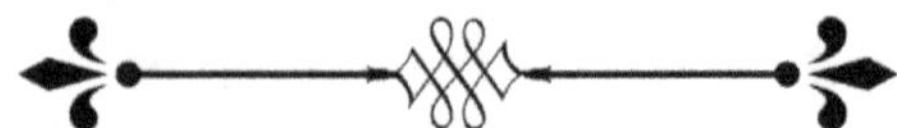

Once you forgive, great changes are going to come in your life. When you begin to live on purpose big things happen. There was a season in my life where I was driven by control, fear, guilt, and dishonesty. Guilt driven people are manipulated by old memories from their past and this sabotages their future. Without a clear purpose you have no foundation. How many times do we make New Year's resolutions and don't keep them? All the time, right? How many of us stick to it? Some do, but I believe there is a solution, and the solution can appear suddenly. It took 18 long years of struggling with my problems, I prayed over and over, and the solution suddenly came. However, in my experience I learned that it could take one prayer to get to your suddenly. This is not always overnight. Faith is about doing our part as well. When we do our part then God can put his super on top of our natural. I am very grateful to the lord! By the grace of God, I've never looked back. You cannot drive looking out the back window. You will crash and die. This is like a dog returning to his vomit! I stayed focused and persevered and so can you. Believe me when I say you can do it.

Strong women win, just like in a horror movie it seems like things are all wrong but in fact they are right! Keep praying and believing, GOD WILL SHOW YOU THE RIGHT WAY! People say dreams do come true but what if they do not? Does that mean you give up on yourself? Just keep pushing and believing and before you know you made it, praise God! I remember being at my lowest at one point in a time in my life I was broken, I barely had enough money to feed my family (4) children I can remember one time I had to choose whether to pay rent or buy groceries, But God made a way every time!

You see God can take your hurt and pain and turn it into victory! The reason why so many people today are living with so much pain is because they are embarrassed or ashamed to share their story. For God's kingdom power to be active in you this requires commitment and for you to live in your truth. This beautiful lady suffered so much pain that caused her to struggle in relationships and self-esteem issues. She dealt with emptiness for years. She always felt like she was alone even when there were people around her. Can you imagine being in a crowded room, everyone sees you and you still feel alone? She would often think about that horrific night, and she would always question herself why did that happen to me? Why was no one there to help me? It seemed like the whole neighborhood was silent. It was a hot summer night, where was everyone? Normally everyone would be outside sitting on their porches, kids riding their bikes, people just standing around having fun, but she wondered where was everyone that night I needed help?

Distractions will come no matter what season. The good part about that is God sees us where we are. God hears our prayers in the middle of the dark and overwhelming nights even when we pray with our hands on our hips. The best news about that is when you are a valued woman who chooses to walk in the fear of God, then it's his job to find and provide the tools you need to get his work done.

This goes back to living a fruitless life. Living a fruitless life means if you have a garden of your own you must bear fruit. A grape orchard that doesn't produce grapes would be pointless. God is always in a constant state of growing us gradually! Like a stem from the root!

You know who and what I'm talking about pertaining to bearing fruit. People and situations, people who challenge you, encourage you, and most importantly those who are not like you. Tough situations that have the most potential to take a nice, pleasant day and turn it into something completely different. For example, a big old cold glass of grape juice! Ha!

I know you say what does that have to do with anything? Listen, it's all wrapped up into one. When you prepare ahead of time and you get your mind centered on God's word, you'll be able to deal with life more effectively. This means any trails or adversities. Here is a quick snapshot of common hazards outside of the happy zone. Now here comes the chili sauce! Yes! Have you ever been disappointed? I'm talking about so disappointed that it scared your soul. Yeah, me too! But I've learned about that was that God did not use me because of who I was but, he used me despite whose I was! He does not look at our performance the way people do. This is a great thing because God standard is absolute perfection. God does not grade us on a curve we can score a 99% with him and still fail the test but his love for us everlasting!

Sometimes everything is not all about. The purpose of your life is far greater than your own personal fulfillment. Let me tell you, peace of mind and your happiness is far greater than anything you'll ever know. If you ever want to know why you were placed on earth, go to God for direction.

It all begins with the creator our God. You were born on purpose, God 's purpose. However, we can't be selfish or self-centered always asking what do I want to do? What do I want to be in life? What are my ambitions or goals for the future? We always skip over just asking God what he wants us to do. The search for the purpose of this life has puzzled people for many years, but why? Simply because we typically begin at the wrong starting point, which is(ourselves). You will not discover your life's meaning by looking within yourself which you probably already tried that. You won't know your purpose but the intervention itself wouldn't be able to tell you either. Only the creator himself can give you the owner's manual. This reveals your purpose. I once got lost on a road trip into the mountains. I stopped and asked for directions, and I was told that you can go through this street to get to the next one. I quickly found out you must start from the other side of the mountain top. WHAT???, I said to myself. That's the way we try to arrange our own life's purpose. We always start out focusing on ourselves. We must begin our life 's purpose with our creator our God.

## Black Woman You have Purpose

We were all created by God, until we understand that our lives will never make sense it is only in God, we will discover our origins. Let that sink in for a while. We must know our identity, our meaning and purpose through this journey. If we take another path, it may lead us to a dead end. In life it's very important to know our purpose here on this earth! You see, most of us use God for our own actualization. What life is really about? We must allow God to use us for his purpose, not our own, always remember that. Know that your life does matter to him! Never give up and go after your goals.

*Clarify your valuables, aim high and figure out what you're good at and go for it. Self-help is no help at all, but self-sacrifice is the way to go.*

I found out that most brilliant philosophers speculate about the meaning of life. Sometimes they even ask, what is the meaning of life? Wow! Fortunately, there is an alternative about speculation and the meaning of life 's purpose, it's called revelation.

After been involved in toxic relationships I felt like I was tripping over my own feet. I kept relying on my own toxic decisions instead of knowing my self-worth and God 's purpose for my life. First, I was down and out about it, but I had to keep going and keep my head lifted high. I kept a smile on my face and a positive perspective about it. This was not easy but with strength from God, I made it through.

# ALECIA TAMEKO

# ALECIA TAMEKO

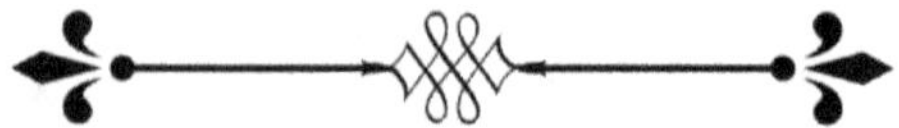

God won't bless you until you release some things and people that are holding you captive. This is not about my journey of what I've been through but my journey as an overcomer. There's a difference between being willing and able. Through the grace of God, I can walk but am I willing to walk away from those that don't serve a purpose for the calling on my life.

November 2021, was the change to my winning season. I had endured a toxic relationship, filled with emotional abuse, resentment, childhood traumas, manipulation, drug use, and infidelity. As a human we want to be loved, and love on others. The problem which can be one-sided comes when a person may have mommy/daddy issues. What does that mean in my opinion, that's when a man/woman did not receive the care that they desired growing up and look for that in their partner. I feel this comes with codependency. I speak from experience. I am one that grew up in a two-parent household and did not experience those issues but because of the way I was raised and the love they shared for one reason or another I attracted men who desired a mother figure and the relationship itself.

Sunday, November 7, 2021, I dropped to my knees and prayed to God to release me from what had been hindering my growth. I said yes Lord I will obey if you guide me and order my steps. That night the man I love, the man I was going to marry, the one I had been with for two years, the man I allowed to take my love for granted left me caged in my own home for days at a time with no means of transportation, watching his children. I'd also began to refer to his children as if I had birthed them. I was taken advantage of, lonely, unheard, misunderstood, devalued and small. I prayed many times before but this moment in time was different. At this time, I had already been stripped. My heart became cold. I became bitter, distant, depressed and withdrawn. I was just a shell of a woman crying for help. Can you believe I had two cars taken totaled. My bills were behind, and my looks had even changed. My health was declining. My cry for help that night was my war cry to get back in the ring and fight like I had never fought before. I needed to be released from captivity. What I know now and did not see then was I was praying for his release as well because he had a death grip on me. I was dying on the inside. My prayer life had ceased. I am no saint, and I can admit to my sins, but I am a praying woman more now than ever. That night changed me. It did not just release me from the torment or what I thought was love. It was a rebirth of the woman I had been fighting to become for years. Before I entered this relationship, I was celibate and on a journey of being renewed. A moment of pleasure and a want to satisfy my flesh turned into two LONG exhausting years. Was it necessary? Maybe. There is always a lesson to be learned. My lesson…

What I know now is, I am more than enough for the man who will love me wholeheartedly. I am enough that I can love me as I grow each day. We like to think freedom comes free, but freedom always comes at a cost. I'm at a point in my life where I no longer allow others to make withdrawals at my expense when no deposits have been made. I take responsibility because some of the situations could have been prevented on my part. I lost who I was because I thought it was love. The win for me is that I allowed myself to grieve another failed relationship and opened my heart to love me the way I deserve to be loved. I speak with authority. I walk with my head high. I no longer feel invisible when I walk in a room. I relocated and I am living in my overflow. That's the message. This is my story. I am a black woman who wins daily because I continue to walk in my truth no matter how scary and ugly it looks to the human eye.

# KEISHA
# "WRITENOW"
# ALLEN

# MS. LOST AND NOW FOUND (The Beginning)
## KEISHA "WRITENOW" ALLEN

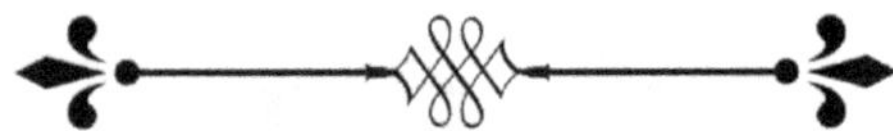

*Author of Worth the Weight: A Love Like No Other*

Thought: Even as I'm writing this chapter, my fears of not being good enough are plaguing me, but I can't stop; won't stop because I know there's someone out there who needs to hear my story.

I'd like to refer to myself as the dreamer who fell off: The talented young woman who had several talents but was afraid to use them. Unlike some of the other amazing women in this anthology, my struggles came from inner demons; the struggle of not feeling I was good enough to ever be able to have people want to listen to my story. You see, I never had a problem with having big dreams. In fact, I knew from an early age that I was supposed to be doing great things; Big dreams, visions beyond my greatest imagination were a blessing and a curse because I had a disease … a major problem; I had a fear of failing. Sprinkle that with the act of not following through and the crippling illness of starting and never finishing; and you have a disaster. I was the dreamer who stopped dreaming, and for me, this was worse than death.

Writing has always been something I've enjoyed. As far back as my elementary grade years, I can remember folding my paper into four parts and turning it into mini books. My imagination was vivid, and I could conjure something up in minutes. In my teens, I began composing my version of a novel, written by yours truly, by hand. I didn't need a typewriter; handwriting by paper and pencil was the way to go. I could sit in my room for hours on end, and just write. I would compose a chapter, then call my best friend and read it to her. She would encourage me to continue, and when she saw me slowing down, she would tell me not to call her again until I had written some more. Unfortunately, even with her push, I got sidetracked.

I can recall my freshman year of high school when I forgot to do my homework assignment; The teacher had given specific instructions: We were supposed to write a short story; it was supposed to be up to five pages, but the teacher only wanted to see that we had at least started and had 2 of the pages finished. What she didn't tell us was that having the 2 pages done by the due date was an A or a 0 kind of deal. The A was the teacher simply checking to see if we'd done the assignment so far. She wasn't even checking to see how good it was. Can I tell you how I silently kicked myself that day for that slip up? I was about to get a 0 for something that I could've done with my eyes closed, but thankfully, a miracle happened for me that day. Although I usually had the unfortunate trend of being called on first because of my last name, the teacher decided to start with the latter part of the alphabet. She started from the back of the class and began to make her way around the room. When I tell you, I whipped out my pencil and started writing in my notebook with warped speed! By the time the teacher made her way to me, I had a fully finished story, just like that. I grinned at her, stuck my little chest out, and proudly presented her with a dope ass story in just minutes. That's how amazing my creative writing skills were.

Then, at some point I lost my way. Careers in the arts were not supported much in my Caribbean family, and by the time I got to college, writing was just a fond memory. I decided to take on a job at UPS and was excited about doing a "real" job, who cares if I didn't enjoy what I was doing. The years that followed were of me aimlessly trying to figure out what I was meant to do. I was told though, that it was OK. It was normal for a college student to not know what they wanted to do in life. But why am I here? I asked, and was shut down with, just do your pre-requisites… you'll figure it out soon enough. I spent the majority of that first year in college, questioning why I was there, and I constantly found myself in the office seeking career counseling. Needless to say, I became a college dropout on academic probation. By the time I got into my twenties, I was working with temp agencies, which led me to health insurance, and let me say, I hated it! I knew there were many avenues in insurance where I could make plenty of money, but it didn't matter. I was flat out bored, miserable, and questioning what I was supposed to be doing with my life.

Most of my thirties were spent much the same way; The most eventful thing I would say is after several years of crippling periods, when I was 33 the doctor discovered a large dermoid cyst on my ovary, and I was ushered into emergency surgery. A dermoid who? I had never heard of that, but the outcome… I lost that ovary. More about that later… I continued to spend much of my time unhappily working jobs that I knew would not take me where I wanted to go. The problem though… I didn't know where that was. With each passing day, I was feeling more and more like my life didn't matter. I wasn't sure what my creator had put me on earth to do, and that's when depression slowly started creeping in. You see, for a dreamer like myself, living without purpose wasn't living. I was existing just to exist, and the worst thing about just existing, is you feel as though you have nothing to live for. And, for me, that was like a death sentence. I see why they say you must hit rock bottom at times to remember who you really are. Because when I was almost 40, I nearly died. No, it wasn't from an illness or an accident, but simply because I … was … lost.

So, here's to almost being 40. Only, instead of going into my 40s hopeful, I was hopeless. At an age when most of my peers were somewhat established, I was still single, living at home, at another job I knew I didn't belong in, I gained 30 unwanted pounds, was having erratic periods, hot flashes, feeling exhausted on most days, had an aunt who was like a mother to me be diagnosed with brain cancer, and I entered a relationship with a narcissist who tried to break me. Remember that ovary I lost at 33? It messed me up and sent me running to see different doctors to see what help I could get from encountering an early menopause. I began seeing an acupuncturist, my gynecologist, and a fertility doctor all at the same time because this is the same time my beautiful aunt fell ill, and I was doing it alone. Several uncomfortable tests later, the doctor diagnosed me with something called PCOS (polycystic ovarian syndrome), and it was something that could've been triggered by the loss of my ovary. If you know anything about PCOS, is it can cause weight gain, mood swings, infertility, and a host of other issues.

During this time, I struggled to get out of bed on most days. I spent time my time depressed about my life, and while I wasn't necessarily suicidal. I found myself telling God that it was OK if I didn't wake up the next morning. I truly needed a miracle, and in 2018, that's just what happened.

Why I'm winning: (Not the End)

In 2018, God allowed me to have enough strength to intentionally search for my purpose. I tuned out the noise and I began to seek with everything inside of me. I journaled, prayed, and meditated daily, and the television wasn't turned on when I went home. I listened to every sermon and podcast I could find. I spent time looking for any and everything positive to put in my spirit, and then I got an email: It simply read, "Do you want to learn to write your book in 4 weeks?" Until this day, I don't know how Tressa "Azarel" Smallwood got my email address, but I'm thankful she did. I signed up for that class on the spot, and my writing journey began again. I began to write my first story. A love, mystery, suspense kind of story. I also started on the follow up to that story when I was forced to stay home during the pandemic. Then, I was blessed to get another job which afforded me the chance to be on the road, and while I enjoyed that for a while, my biggest breakthrough happened when I was home and couldn't go on the road for ten months due to the pandemic. I was able to write my second book, Worth the Weight: A Love Like No Other, which is about a woman navigating career, relationships, self-love, weight, and finding her true purpose (sound familiar)? Worth the Weight became the first book I self-published through my publishing company, Kreative Kreations Publishing, which I started in 2020, and it has become a bestseller across several platforms.

No, it hasn't been easy, and I have to admit that I'm always doing it scared, but hey; I'm doing it! Hopefully, I can inspire someone (young or older) that it's not too late to find, follow, and live your purpose. Never discount your wins as small as they may seem to you. I'm an example of what can happen if you allow yourself to find that spark deep down in your soul, and light that fire. I invite you to take the first step on your journey, no matter how scary it may seem. That situation you're in does not have to be your forever, but it's up to you to make that dream a reality, and if you don't know what your purpose is, it's not too late to find and fulfill it, because someone is waiting to hear from you.

# LIEASHA OFFORD "THE WOLF"

# LIEASHA OFFORD THE WOLF

Many don't want to expose desperation, whether good or bad. I must warn you in advance that this place is likened to a haunted house, with mirrors of Illusions and the gate keeper is deception.

I remember waking up one day, feeling very strange and misplaced. I suppose it was due to so many events that I witnessed as a child, and unknowingly suppressed. Mother and father getting a divorce, and him not being around left me scared and mentally aggravated and moments of fear would overwhelm me, that secretly I would crawl under my bed and hide from everyone. I didn't feel safe, something was missing. Mother was great and did her best covering her children and made the best decision to cover us in her form of beauty, however a father covering is also needed and as a child I always longed for that baby girl relationship with dad, I was so desperate to fill that irritable void. Life happened I was now excepting the voices in the house no one heard but myself and the voices would "state your fat, you're not pretty, no one wants you, remember even your aunt calls you EVIL." I would be so tired and sleepy not being able to focus, at school, I even picked a fight, yes, my garments were changing.

I began having unusual dreams and visions. Mentally physically and emotionally I began seeing and yielding toward and to unnatural things and behaviors. During those times I remember just wanting my grandma Ruth. However, I couldn't drive at the time to make a choice to go visit her and tell her how I was feeling. My grandma was a great listener, and in my opinion, she was my destiny helper. Growing up in a house where there was no daddy, infected and affected me. Even seeing that my wonderful mother was struggling to do her best, bothered me because I knew she needed help. I decided unconsciously to suffer and not express myself because in my head the voices were telling me that my mother loved the brothers of mine more than me and they needed her more. One day, I went to hug my mother after seeing my older brother hug her, thinking that mom would embrace me the same. My mother pushed me away. So, growing up, I never tried giving my mom a hug again. There were many times in my childhood where mother would constantly repeat, be it good or bad, mother would say "You look just like your dad." or she would say "You got ugly ways just like your dad." Let me explain. My dad was very abusive to my mother and did horrible things to my mom, sister and brothers. He was a thief, liar and a functional alcoholic. The list goes on. As I grew up, I suppressed everything still having no sense of truth to share what was happening. All I knew was shame, rejection, told to be quiet and I better not say nothing. As mother took on night shift, so did everything else that love to play in the dark, especially with young children or simply put young teens and even babies. With my brothers and eldest sister being home with me they were off doing whatever. While everyone was distracted the gate keeper gazed opportunity and invited a group of strong men into our house. These strong men never travelled alone. If they felt like you had their kind of goods, they gave themselves permission to come claim what they felt belonged to them. Strangely enough, they would show up but stay hidden until others showed up who were stronger than them. Then it was a battle of illusions and performance making room for occupancy. Sometimes without warning, I would shut my room door and go hide under the bed. It appeared to be a safe place to shut out noise and suppressed hurt. I would say "I want my daddy," I want my daddy," then began to cry silently as I could grasping my mouth. Eventually I would come out and no one knew till this day. I would stay in the house all day and at night I would get dressed so pretty and sit on the porch, one of my cousins still jokes about it saying at family outdoor functions. "You know sister Lieasha don't like the sun on her, she not coming out until it gets dark." Those words didn't hurt so I would laugh and feel affirmed because it was true. In a strange way it made me feel safe that my family knew. Well at least that part.

## THE SITUATION

My situation had gotten worse, as I stated early on in previous chapter, I would only go on the porch. I would sit in the house and see how kids were dating. Even in school, seeing as though I didn't realize the extreme of my self-isolation. It turned into self-rejection. I would just go through the motions of pretending I was happy, and some people loved me while others thought I was just weird. Either way, it didn't matter to me what others thought because secretly I didn't feel pretty. Eventually, I truly did not have a real social life. I was afraid. Fear, my hands and my body became my problematic, compromised, and complicated relationship. This was a dangerous comfort zone. How could this have happened? The wrong opportunity attracted unseen opportunist. They watched everything and studied secretly everything about me. From childhood, even now as I type, they're watching and listening. No matter what, I'm determined to help someone so let's continue. First my mind, then ears, my tongue, my feet, my hands and eventually my mind, soul, body and spirit. Let me tell you that these strongmen that came into my house were playing for keeps. They literally told me to commit suicide by drinking and taking pills. They knew that I was not a drinker, but because the strongmen knew my dad was, they tried using my hands in the same way to kill myself. Yes, I attempted and was unsuccessful because that night a gospel channel was on and the minister kept "saying put that bottle down and mentioning Jesus." The suicidal thoughts didn't go away. For some reason they went into hiding to conjure up.

Another plan of death again involving my hands. Every day I would turn my attention to the special facilities called the bathroom. After eating anything I would go into the bathroom stick my finger down my throat and throw up everything. Who would know? There were so many things unseen happening with me every day. The only people that I grew up with in my household did not have a clue. I was dying before their eyes. Were they blinded because there were more strongmen assigned to them in our household? Listen, I went from 143 pounds to 102 pounds. Again, I already didn't feel pretty. The last thing you want to do is get FAT. The strongmen would remind me of this every day and every second. I was walking dead and didn't feel anything or realize it. I forgot to mention that I would wear big clothes, because every time I saw myself in the mirror I saw fat face, body, ugly everywhere on me. PAUSE HERE......TO BE CONTINUED. I had to stop writing for a moment, while writing I heard a horrid voice state, "You better not write that!" Instantly I was shaken, stopped typing and called my coach Prophetess Dr. Evette Young. I explained to her what happened. She comforted me and supported me. She told me f I needed to stop and close my computer for a moment then that would be good. She prayed over me and now after a couple of months of fighting to return to this process, my overwhelmingness has been put to death. I have greater strength to continue. The reality is that this my first time writing in such depth. Not only have I shed many tears but realized also that this part of my deliverance does not belong solely to me alone but, someone else. I had to fast, pray and missed days of work due to illness and struggles within to return. This process has cost much. Nevertheless, my obedience to God to serve his people to be set free for real is worth everything. In these end times we need real power to be set free and stay free. Families must come into all truth through the Holy Spirit, to turn that which has been suppressed hidden dysfunctional secrets into balanced, healed and healthy lives. We must have the courage to become involved in our own deliverance if not for ourselves then LET'S DO IT FOR OUR CHILDREN AND LOVED ONES. I want to end this part with what has helped me throughout this process. Opening myself up to remembering to utilize the GIFT OF REPENTANCE…. a gift that God gave to us all, and like any gift given you must properly with respect embrace it. In court they say you must tell the whole truth and nothing but the truth so help you God. You must repent even in situations where you did not know the severity of the matter. You know

now and now you can rejoice in what you know because now that which use to torment and make you feel guilty now has no more power over you. You can move forward in your process of obtaining true freedom in your mind, soul and spirit. Just remember, in these end times, we need real power to deal with our flesh and real enemies. They may be invisible to some but I'm here to tell you they do manifest in human form through objects, word curses, and so much more. We must AWAKEN OUR SUPERNATURAL APPETITE AND SENSES. Please, I beg you to take heed to these words and do not be left behind. We are in a real war and whether you like it or not The Lord Jesus Christ, The King of Kings, The Lord of Lords is coming back for his bride without spot or wrinkle. Invest in your life and do not be found sleep and a casualty of war. Hopefully you have ears to hear, and your heart not hardened after reading this. Know this, no matter what the devil or darkness may present, it cannot create nor can offer you ETERNAL LIFE.

If you're reading this book, it's not by some fluke, trust the process. Whenever I get to this part of where I began to expose the wolf and its identity, now I sense their fear. Literally you know when you sense a presence but you're the only one naturally in that space, well know that this time I won't shut down. There are also my guardian angels present and a huge warring angel with me. Before I write or study I always practice inviting the Holy Spirit to breath upon me and what I write and study. The Holy Ghost fire will consume any evil and all like manner thereof and that there be no backlash backfire or counterattack of any kind from darkness. I'm at a place where I will not tolerate evil. Be that in or around me. At times I just have no desire to eat, I'm not even hungry and my body shifts into a fast. Nevertheless, I am cover by the blood of Jesus.

## BLESSED AS A BLACK WOMAN

My journey as a black woman, saved and serving God as I know how has truly brought me through many situations. Some things I'm proud of and some things I'm not. This is the joy of experiencing the favor of God truly and undeniably. I want to encourage black women to never give up in your journey of living a healthy, spirit filled life and whatever God has called you to. Life may not always seem exciting and there will be some days that may be sad or gloomy but remind yourself that you were made in his image and likeness. Nothing, not nothing can truly stop you when you are created with power and integrity. Black women stand up and take your place. Be Blessed.

WE PRAY YOU HAVE ENJOYED
THESE AMAZING STORIES FROM BLACK
WOMEN ACROSS THE GLOBE.


BE SURE TO FOLLOW US ON SOCIAL
MEDIA AND VISIT OUR WEBSITE

WWW.BLACKWOMENWIN.COM